CUBA

Welcome and thank you for purchasing my cookbook. For some time I have wanted to make a Cuban cookbook to share some of the same kind of recipes my abuela cooked for us growing up. I dedicate this to my abuela who was born and raised in Key West Florida and her abuelos who came here from Cuba back in 1868 and 1885. In here you will find over 30 recipes from some of my favorite Cuban style appetizers, meat dishes, desserts and drinks. I hope you enjoy them as much as I do and hope you have fun making them!

AF439751

TABLE OF CONTENTS

APPETIZERS

Fried Sweet Plantains

Ingredients

- 3 plantains (ripe & soft)
- oil

Preparation

When buying, select very ripe soft almost black plantains.

Remove the peel and slice diagonally on a slant into 1 inch slices.

Heat oil to 350 degrees in a pan.

Fry plantains until golden brown, turning them as they cook.

Place on paper towel to drain excess oil.

Serves 6

Bollos De Frijoles (Black-eye Peas Fritters)

Ingredients

- 2 cups of dried black-eyed peas
- 4 garlic cloves, crushed
- 1/4 teaspoon hot sauce
- 1 teaspoon of salt
- Oil for frying

Preparation

Cover the black-eye peas with cold water and let them soak overnight.

Drain but reserve the water. Remove the skins by rubbing peas between the palms of your hands. Making sure the peas are completely skinless.

Puree the peas in a food processor until as fine as cornmeal (or use a food grinder, which will take several grindings). Add the garlic, hot sauce, salt and about ½ cup of the reserved water. Mix until the mixture is light like cake batter. Adding additional water it if necessary.

Cover and refrigerate for about 1-2 hours.
Heat the oil to 350 degrees.
Drop in teaspoonfuls of the mixture, a few at a time. Deep-fry for 1 to 2 minutes or until golden brown.

Drain on paper towels.
Makes about 40.

Conch Fritters

Ingredients

- 1/2 cup chopped sweet bell pepper
- 1/2 cup chopped red bell pepper
- 1 chopped sweet onion
- 3 eggs beaten
- 1 teaspoon salt
- 1 teaspoon black pepper
- 1 teaspoon baking powder
- 1 tablespoon Tabasco hot sauce
- 2 pounds ground conch
- 2 tablespoons white vinegar
- 2 cups of flour
- 6 cups oil - For deep frying fritters in

Preparation

Mix together the conch, onion, green bell pepper, red bell pepper, eggs, hot sauce, vinegar, baking powder, salt and black pepper.

Add the flour a little at a time and continue to stir until all flour is incorporated.

Heat the oil to 350 degrees.

Drop in teaspoonfuls of the mixture, a few at a time. Deep-fry for 1 to 2 minutes or until golden brown.

Drain on paper towels.

Can be served with tartar, cocktail or a favorite dipping sauce.

Smoked Fish Dip

Ingredients

- 16 oz smoked white fish
- 1/2 cup mayo
- 1 block cream cheese (room temp)
- 3 jalapenos (no seeds)
- 3 tablespoon Old Bay seasoning
- 2 lime

Preparation

Room temp your cream cheese.

Flake fish and pulse in a food processor.

In a large bowl combine the cream cheese, mayo, jalapenos, Old Bay seasoning, juice from 2 limes and the smoked fish.

Mix it all up and chill.

Serve with chips or crackers.

Guacamole

Ingredients

- 3 avocados (large/ripe)
- 1 tomato, medium (seeded and diced)
- 1/2 white onion (diced)
- 1/2 cup cilantro,1/3 of bunch (finely chopped)
- 1/2 teaspoon sea salt
- 1/4 teaspoon black pepper, freshly ground
- 3 tablespoon lime juice

Preparation

Pit your 3 avocados into a mixing bowl. Coursely mash with a potato masher.

Squeeze lime juice directly over the top of the avocados to prevent browning.

Add your diced tomatoes, cilantro and onion. Season with salt and peppper.

Stir to combine all ingredients and serve.

Crab Cakes

Ingredients

- 1 lb. lump crabmeat
- 1 onion, small (minced)
- 1/2 cup sweet bell pepper (minced)
- 1/2 cup red bell pepper (minced)
- 1/4 cup celery (minced)
- 2 eggs (beaten)
- 1 teaspoon Old Bay seasoning
- 1 teaspoon hot sauce
- 1 cup cracker meal
- 1/4 cup parsley (chopped)
- Butter or olive oil
- 1-2 lemons

Preparation

Saute your onion, celery and peppers in a little butter or olive oil for about 3 minutes.

In a bowl break up the crabmeat.
Add the onion mixture to the crab along with the eggs, seasoning, parsley, hot sauce and cracker meal.

Mix gently and form into patties.
Pan-fry in butter or olive oil until browned.

Serve with lemon wedges.

Hot Crab Dip

Ingredients

- 1 lb. cream cheese (softened)
- 1 sour cream (8oz container)
- 1 lb. crabmeat
- 1 onion (small & minced)
- 1 tablespoon red bell pepper (minced)
- 1/4 cup mayo
- 2 tablespoon butter
- 1 teaspoon Old Bay seasoning
- Shredded cheese (cheddar and/ or parm)
- Salt & black pepper to taste
- Scallions for garnish
- Crackers

Preparation

Room temp your cream cheese
Preheat oven to 350 degrees.

Saute the onion and red pepper in butter until soft.

Add the crabmeat, seasoning, mayo and stir well.

Stir in sour cream.
Salt & pepper to taste.

Spread in baking dish and sprinkle with shredded cheese.

Bake for aprox 20-30 minutes until golden and bubbly.

Top with a few scallions if desired.

Serve with crackers and/or celery.

SALADS

Avocado & Tomato Salad

Ingredients

- 2 avocados (large,firm,ripe)
- 4 tomatoes (large, ripe)
- 2 teaspoons lime juice
- 1/4 cup olive oil
- 3 tablespoons wine vinegar
- 1 teaspoon salt
- 1/2 teaspoon black pepper

Preparation

Cut avocados into chunks and place in salad bowl.
Cut tomatoes into wedges and add to salad bowl with the avocados.

Combine lime juice, olive oil, vinegar, salt and pepper and pour over tomatoes and avocados in bowl.

Mix lightly.

Island Cole Slaw

Ingredients

- 1 cabbage, medium (chopped finely)
- 1 onion, small (chopped finely)
- 4 celery stalks (chopped finely)
- 1 large carrot (grated)
- 1/2 sweet bell pepper (chopped finely)
- 1 cup mango or pineapple
- 1 tablespoon salt
- 1/2 teaspoon black pepper
- 2 teaspoons sugar
- 1/4 cup olive oil
- 1/4 cup cider vinegar
- 2 cups mayo

Preparation

Thoroughly mix all ingredients, except for the mayo.

Once mixed then add mayo and stir until creamy.

Tropical Fruit Salad

Ingredients

- 2 large cans fruit cocktail
- 2 large cans sliced peaches
- 3 cans mandarin oranges
- 1 jar maraschino cherries (cut in half)
- 2 cans crushed pineapple
- 1 large container Cool Whip
- 1 cup sour cream
- 1 can condensed milk
- 1 pkg. coconut (8oz)
- 1 pkg. walnuts (8oz) (chopped)
- *Peaches & Oranges can be substituded for a different fruit

Preparation

Drain your fruit cocktail, peaches, oranges, pineapple and place in bowl.

Don't drain the cherries.

Add the coconut, Cool Whip, sour cream, condensed milk, cherries, nuts. Add a little bit of the cherry juice to add color to your salad.

Stir/Fold until well blended.

Chill through aprox 6 hours and serve.

Six Cup Summer Salad

Ingredients

- 1 cup miniature marshmallows
- 1 cup pineapple tidbits
- 1 cup flakes coconut
- 1 cup oranges (cut into small pieces)
- 1/2 cup purple and/or green grapes (optional)
- 1/2 cup maraschino cherries
- 1 cup sour cream

Preparation

Mix all your ingredients together.

Chill for 1-2 hours.

Add more sourcream if necessary and serve.

RICE VEGETABLE
& PASTA
PAGE 14

Black Beans & Rice

Ingredients

- 12 ounces dried black beans
- 4 1/2 cups of water
- 3 medium onions (chopped)
- 2 green peppers (chopped)
- 5 cloves garlic (minced)
- 1 cup olive oil
- 4 teaspoon salt
- 2 bay leaves
- 1 teaspoon oregano
- Ground pepper to taste
- 6 cups cooked white rice

Preparation

Wash beans well and put in a covered pot. Cover beans with water, enough to cover them. Add 2 teaspoons of salt and soak overnight.

The next day simmer the beans in the same water they soaked overnight in.

While beans are beginning to boil, pour oil into a frying pan with the onion and peppers. Saute until tender. Add your garlic, bay leaves and oregano to the onions and peppers and cook for about 5 mins.

Add the cooked peppers and onions mixture to your black beans.

Season with the remaining salt and pepper.

Cook the black beans until theynare tender, aprox 1 1/2 - 2 Hours. Adding a little more water to it if necessary. Boil beans gently and very little to prevent breaking of the skins.

When done you can serve seperate with white rice or over white rice topped with chopped raw onions.

Yellow Rice

Ingredients

- 4 cups white rice
- 3 tablespoon olive oil
- 1 teaspoon cumin
- 1 bay leaf
- 2 teaspoon salt
- 2 teaspoon bijol
- 1 garlic clove (crushed)
- Parsley to garnish

Preparation

Rinse your rice until water runs clear.

Place rice in pot or a rice cooker and add water to cover rice by 2 inches. *Rice Cookers follow instructions as to the amount of water to add.

Add the cumin, bay leaf, salt, bijol, garlic and stir.

Add olive oil and stir.

Bring your rice to a boil then reduce heat to low and cover. Cook for about 20 minutes or until water is absorbed.

Fluff with fork and serve. Parsley for garnish.

Easy Stuffed Potatoes

Ingredients

- 8 peeled boiled potatoes
- 1 lb. ground chuck
- 1/2 cup onion (chopped)
- 2 fresh garlic cloves (crushed)
- 1 tablespoon olive oil
- 1 cup tomato sauce
- 1/2 cup water
- Salt and Pepper to taste

Preparation

Boil potatoes in salted water for 8 minutes.

Meanwhile, saute the garlic and onions in the olive oil. Add ground beaf to the sauted garlic and onions and cook until browned.

When potatoes are cool enough to handle, core out the middle to accommodate the beef.

Chop up the cored out potatoe pieces and add to the beef mixture along with 1/4 of the tomato sauce. Stir and add salt and pepper to taste.

Fill potatoes with meat mixture and place in pan. If you have any leftover meat mixture put the remaining over the potatoes.

Mix the remaining tomato sauce with the water and pour over the potatoes. Cover and simmer until tender.

Spaghetti and Meatballs

Ingredients

- 2 lbs. ground chuck
- 4 slices of bread
- 1 cup milk
- 2 eggs (beaten)
- 1 cup parsley (chopped)
- 3 garlic cloves (finely minced)
- 1 cup parmesan cheese
- 2 teaspoon salt
- 1 teaspoon black pepper
- 1 jar of spaghetti sauce
- 1 lb cooked spaghetti

Preparation

Preheat oven to 425 degrees.

Soak 4 slices of bread in 1 cup milk.

Combine the meat with garlic, parsley, eggs, soaked bread, parmesan cheese, salt and pepper.

Once all mixed roll into golf size meatballs and place on baking sheet with parchment paper.

Bake meatballs for 15-20 minutes.

When done in the oven add to your simmering sauce on low for 15 minutes

Serve over hot spaghetti and sprinkle with extra parmesan cheese.

MEAT DISHES
PAGE 19

Picadillo (Meat Hash)

Ingredients

- 1 lb. ground chuck
- 3 tablespoons olive oil
- 1/4 lb. ground ham
- 1/2 cup onion (chopped)
- 1 tablespoon galic (minced)
- 1/4 cup sweet bell pepper (chopped)
- 1 teaspoon dried oregano
- 1 1/4 teaspoon gound cumin
- 1 bay leaf
- 1 cup tomato sauce
- 1/4 cup vino seco (dry white wine)
- 1/4 cup raisins
- 1/4 cup green olives (chopped)
- 1 teaspoon capers

Preparation

Saute the onion, green pepper and garlic in the olive oil.

Add the ground chuck to mixture and cook until it begins to brown.

Add the ham, oregano, cumin, and the bay leaf. Stir.

Stir in tomato sauce, olives, capers, vino seco (dry white wine) and raisins.

Cover and simmer on low for about 15 minutes.

Serve with or over white rice and a side of plantains.
Serves 4

Ropa Vieja (Old Clothes)

Ingredients

- 1 flank steak
- 8 cups water
- 1 carrot (chopped)
- 4 garlic cloves (crushed)
- 1/2 sweet bell pepper (sliced lengthwise)
- 1 1/2 cup of sofrito (Goya brand)
- 1/2 cup meat broth (reserved from cooking steak)
- 1/4 cup vino seco (dry white wine)
- 1/4 cup sweet peas
- 2 oz jar of pimiento strips
- 10 pimiento stuffed green olives
- 1 tablespoon olive oil
- 1 can tomato sauce

Preparation

Boil the flank steak in a 4 quart pot with about 2 quarts of water with the carrot, onion, garlic, and green pepper for about 15 minutes. Reduce heat to medium-low, cover and cook for about 2 hours or until meat is tender. *Pressure cooker time is 1 hour*

Remove meat and allow to cool. **Reserve a 1/2 cup of Meat Broth**

Shred meat into thread like strips.

Place shredded meat in a pan with sofrito, olive oil, meat broth, olives, tomato sauce, vino seco and peas. Salt to taste and cook for about 15 minutes.

Pour in juice from the jar of pimientos. Add 1/2 of the pimiento strips and mix.

Arrange meat on a platter and place the remaining pimiento stips on top to garnish.

Serve with or over white rice and side of plantains.

Serves 3-4

Fried Steak
(Palomilla Steak)

Ingredients

- 4 top sirloin or palomilla steak (1/4 inch thick)
- 1 tablespoon garlic (crushed)
- 2 tablespoon sour orange juice(or 1 tablespoon orange juice and tablespoon lime juice)
- 1 onion (thinly sliced into rings)
- 1/4 teaspoon salt
- 1/2 cup onion (chopped)
- 1/2 cup fresh parsley (chopped)
- 1/4 cup olive oil
- 1 lime cut into wedges

Preparation

Place steaks in a shallow pan and sprinkle with the minced garlic, juice, onion rings and salt. Cover steaks and let marinate in the refrigerator for about 30 minutes before frying them.

Heat oil in frying pan to high heat. Fry steaks one or two at a time with a share of the onion rings until they are browned.

Mix a side dish of the uncooked chopped onions and parsley mixed together. Sprinkled it over the steaks along with a squeeze of fresh lime.

Serve with black beans and rice with a side of plantains.
Serves 4

Breaded Steak
(Bistec Empanizado)

Ingredients

- 4 top round or cubesteak (1/4 inch thick)
- 1 cup onion (thinly sliced into rings)
- 1 tablesspoon fresh garlic (minced)
- 4 eggs (beaten)
- 4 cups cracker meal
- 1/4 teaspoon salt
- 1 lime cut into wedges
- 4 cups corn oil

Preparation

Sprinkle steaks with salt and rub meat with fresh garlic.

Marinate in the fridge for a few hours.
Dip steaks, one at a time, through the egg first then cracker meal. (when your breading the steaks make sure you press down with the palm of your hand adhering the breading to the meat)

Heat corn oil to 350 degrees and fry each steak until golden brown.
Serve with sliced onion and fresh lime wedges. Black beans, rice and plantains go well with this dish.
Serves 4

Stuffed Potato (Papas Rellena)

Ingredients

- 1 cup leftover picadillo
- 3 cups plain mashed potatoes
- 2 eggs (beaten)
- 4 cups bread crumbs
- 6 cups corn oil

Preparation

Put about 1-1 1/2 tablespoon of potato in the palm of your hand. Shape it into a thick patty, making an indentation in the middle. Put 1/2 tablespoon of picadillo in the center and cover with more potato.

Shape into a ball, making sure the meat stays in the middle. Coat in egg and roll in bread crumbs.

Fry in 350 degree oil until golden brown.

Drain on paper towel and serve.

Cuban Mix Sandwich
(Sanguche Cubano)

Ingredients

- 1 loaf cuban bread
- 1 lb. sweet ham
- 1 lb. roast pork
- 1/2 lb. swiss cheese
- Dill pickle slices
- Mustard
- Mayo
- Butter

Preparation

Cut bread into 4 pieces. Slice open lengthwise.

Place ham, pork and cheese in layers along 1/2 of the sliced bread.

Add the pickle slices.

Spread on the top of the bread with mustard and mayo to taste and close sandwich.

Coat the top of the bread with butter.

Toast the sandwich on a panini press, pressing down as it is toasting.

Place sandwich on a plate and cut diagonally lengthwise.

Enjoy with some plantain chips.

DESSERTS
PAGE 26

Caramel Flan

Ingredients

- **1 can sweetened condensed milk**
- **1 can evaporated milk**
- **5 eggs (large)**
- **1 teaspoon pure vanilla extract**
- **1 1/2 cups sugar**
- **1 pkg cream cheese (room temp)**

Preparation

Room temp your cream cheese.

Preheat oven to 350 degrees.

In a heavy bottom saucepan heat 1/2 cup of sugar over medium-low heat stirring constantly until sugar melts into a golden caramel.
Coat the bottom and sides of a 2 quart baking dish. The caramel will cool into a hard candy.

Mix all the remaining ingredients well in a bowl.

Pour mixture into baking dish and bake in a Bain Marie (place dish in a larger pan to be filled with water).

Bake for 1 hour, remove from oven and cool.
Place dish in refrigerator overnight (this will liquefy the hard caramel).
Loosen the sides with a knife, place a deep dish plate over the flan and flip.
Pour the caramel over the top.
Serves 6-8

Custard (Natilla)

Ingredients

- 3 cups whole milk
- 1/2 lemon rind
- 1 stick cinnamon
- 4 tablespoons cornstarch
- 1/2 cup water
- 1/2 cup sugar
- 4 egg yolks
- 1 teaspoon pure vanilla extract
- Cinnamon to taste

Preparation

In a small saucepan, heat 1 cup milk, lemon rind and cinnamon stick until boiling and then remove from heat.

Dissolve cornstarch in the water.

In a large saucepan, mix the remaining cold milk and cornstarch solution.

Mix sugar and egg yolks together and slowly stir into cold milk.

Strain the cup of hot milk to remove lemon rind, cinnamon stick and any particles.

Now, add hot milk to cold milk mixture and heat over medium heat until thick.

Stir constantly and remove from heat when thickened.

Add vanilla extract and mix well. Pour into individual serving cups.

Sprinkle tops with cinnamon to taste and refrigerate until chilled.
Serves 4

Banana Cream Pie
(Pastel De Coco)

Ingredients

- 2 cups whole milk
- 3 eggs
- 3 tablespoons corn starch
- 2 teaspoons sugar
- 1 teaspoon vanilla
- Pinch of salt
- 2 teaspoons water
- 3 bananas
- 1 pre-baked pie crust

Preparation

Preheat oven to 300 degrees.

Line a 9 inch pie pan with your favorite pie crust.

Heat milk.

Beat egg yolks, add sugar, corn starch, salt, water and mix well.

When the milk boils add mixture and stir until thick.
Remove from heat, add vanilla, and cool.

Cut bananas into thin slices and place in baked pie crust.

When other mixture is cool, spread over bananas.

Beat the egg white with sugar to taste until stiff peaks form.
Spread on top and brown in a 300 degree oven.

Sponge Cake

Ingredients

- 2 egg whites
- 2 egg yolks
- 4 tablespoons hot water
- 3/4 cup sugar
- 1 cup flour
- 1 1/2 teaspoon baking powder
- Zest of one lime
- Lime juice from one lime

Preparation

Preheat oven to 350 degrees.

Beat egg whites until stiff and add half of the sugar.

Add hot water to yolks and beat until thick, then add remaining sugar and lime juice and zest gradually, while beating constantly.

Add egg whites and fold in flour (mixed and sifted with baking powder).

Pour into deep cake pan and bake for 35 minutes.

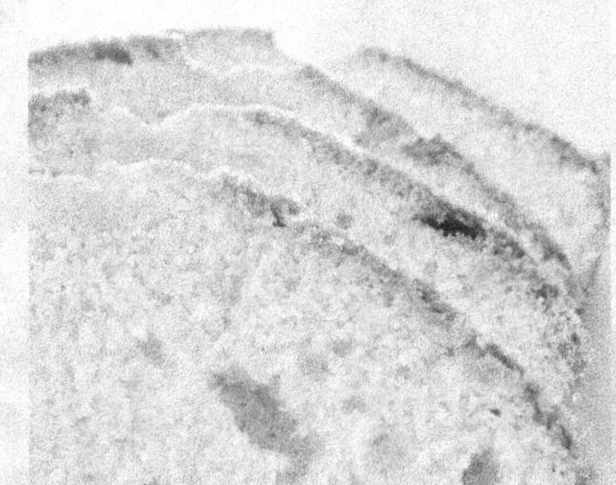

Guava Turnovers

Ingredients

- 1 pkg. guava paste
- 1 pkg. empanada rounds *
- 1 egg (beaten)
- Butter
- Powdered sugar

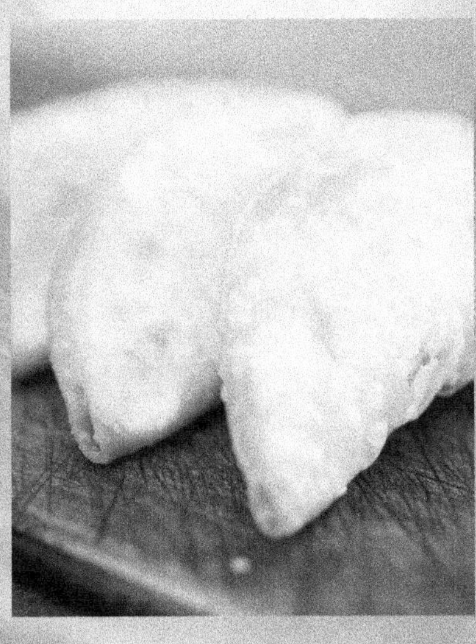

Preparation

Preheat oven to 350 degrees.

Chop up the guava paste.

Place a mound of guava in the center of an empanada round with a dot of butter.

Fold over and press together the empanada round.

Brush the top with egg and sprinkle with sugar.

Place on a cookie sheet and bake until golden brown. Sprinkle with powdered sugar if desired.

-You can substitute the guava paste for another choice of fruit.

* If you cannot find empanada rounds at your grocer's freezer, any pie crust will do, just use a glass to cut out the rounds.*

Drunk Pound Cake

Ingredients

- 1 pound cake
- 1/2 teaspoon cinnamon
- 1 cup rum or brandy
- 1 cup sugar
- 1 cup water

Preparation

Cut the pound cake in slices about a inch thick.

Place in a large flat dish or individual dishes for serving.

Sprinkly with cinnamon and pour over each slice 3-4 tablespoons of rum or brandy. Let sit.

When ready to serve, pour simple syrup over the cake.

Simple Syrup: Add sugar to water and boil for about 10 minutes.

DRINK

Mojito

Piña Colada

The Cuba Libre

Ingredients

- 2 ounce rum
- 3 ounce coca cola
- 1 lime (cut into wedges)
- Ice

Preparation

Fill glass with ice and squeeze a lime wedge and put in glass.

Pour 2 ounce of rum and 3 ounces of cola in glass and garnish with a lime.

Mojito

Ingredients

- 10 fresh mint leaves
- 1 lime (cut into wedges)
- 2 ounces white rum
- Club soda
- Simple syrup*
- Ice

Preparation

Place mint leaves and a lime wedge into a glass and use a muddler to crush the mint and lime wedge to release the oils and juice.

Add 2 more lime wedges and 2-3 tablespoons of simple syrup and muddle again.

Add ice 3/4 way full. Pour rum over ice and add club soda.

Stir to taste and garnish with lime wedge and a mint leaf.

*Simple Syrup: Add 1/2 cup sugar to 1/2 cup water and boil for about 10 minutes, allow to cool.

Pina Colada

Ingredients

- 4 ounces coconut rum
- 2 ounces pineapple juice
- 4 ounces Pina Colada mix
- 1/2 cup vanilla bean ice cream
- 1 1/2 cup ice
- Fresh pineapple for garnish

Preparation

Place all the ingredients in a blender and blend until smooth and creamy.

Pour into glass and garnish with fresh pineapple.

Banana Daiquiri

Ingredients

- 2 ounces of dark rum
- 1/2 ounce fresh lime juice
- 1/2 banana (ripe & thinly sliced)
- 1 teaspoon sugar
- Ice
- Slice of banana for garnish

Preparation

Place all ingredients in the blender.

Blend for about 30 seconds.

Stir mixture and add a few ice cubes.

Blend for another 30 seconds.

Garnish with a fresh slice of banana.

Limeade

Ingredients

- 1 cup fresh lime juice
- 4 cups water
- Ice
- Fresh mint
- Fresh cherries*
- Sugar and/or honey

Preparation

Chill glasses.
Combine the fresh lime juice and water.

Add sugar and/or honey to taste.

Fill chilled glasses 1/2 with ice and pour.

Garnish with mint and cherries.

*If fresh cherries are not available then substitute with maraschino cherries

Thank You
For Your
Support

I Truly Appreciate Your
Business And Hope You
Enjoyed Each Of The Recipes!

https://weberbookpublishing.com/

Weber Book
PUBLISHING

On behalf of Weber Book
Publishing, we wanted to say
thank you for your purchase.